One day at the Taiwan Land Bank Dinosaur Museum

to Jēkabs forever

Copyright

First published in the UK in 2021 by The Emma Press Ltd
Text and artwork copyright © Elīna Eihmane 2021

All rights reserved.

The right of Elīna Eihmane to be identified as the creator of this work has been asserted by her in accordance with the Copyright, Designs and Patents Act 1988.

ISBN 978-1-912915-66-8

A CIP catalogue record of this book is available from the British Library.

Printed and bound in the UK by The Holodeck, Birmingham.

theemmapress.com
hello@theemmapress.com
Birmingham, UK

One day at the Taiwan Land Bank Dinosaur Museum

ELĪNA EIHMANE

THE EMMA PRESS

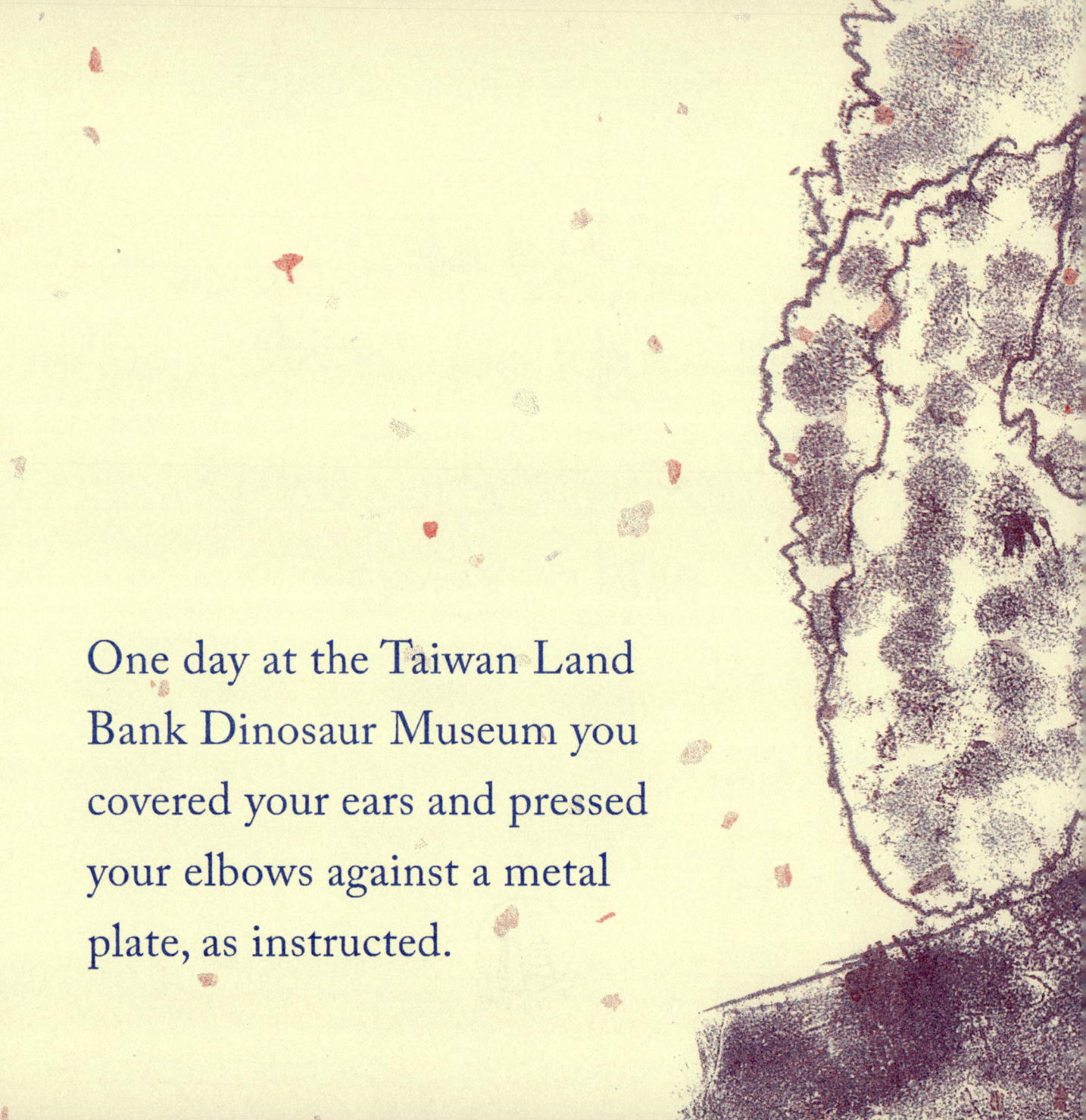

One day at the Taiwan Land Bank Dinosaur Museum you covered your ears and pressed your elbows against a metal plate, as instructed.

With all that shaking, trembling and rumbling, there it was: a whale song ran through your body.

A feeling moved.

I bet it felt like when you were a tiny little human living inside of me, and all the sadness of the journey out.

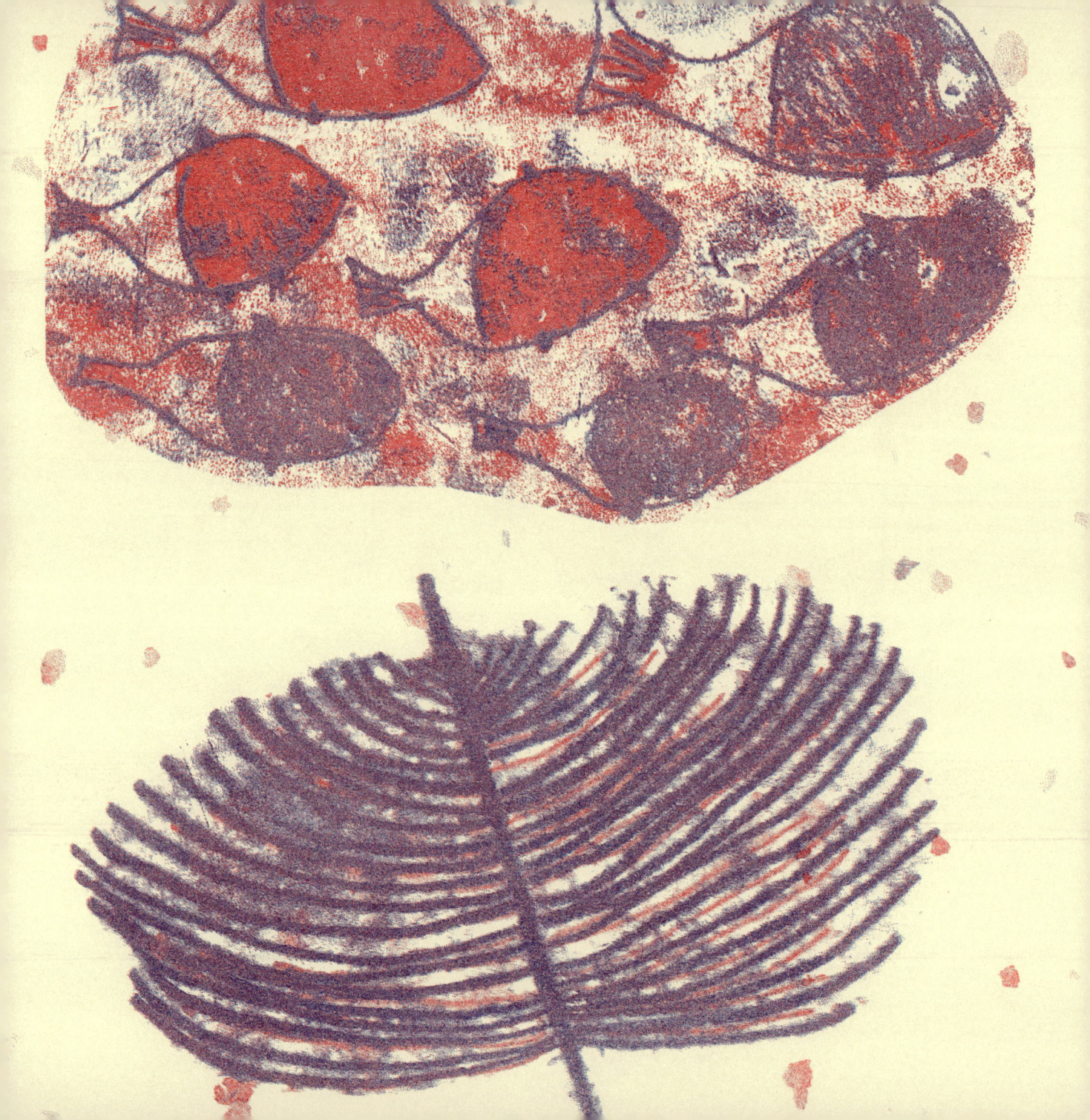

It was so comfortable having you live inside. You were my baby. It must have felt so safe to be so close. It must have been so hard to be dragged out.

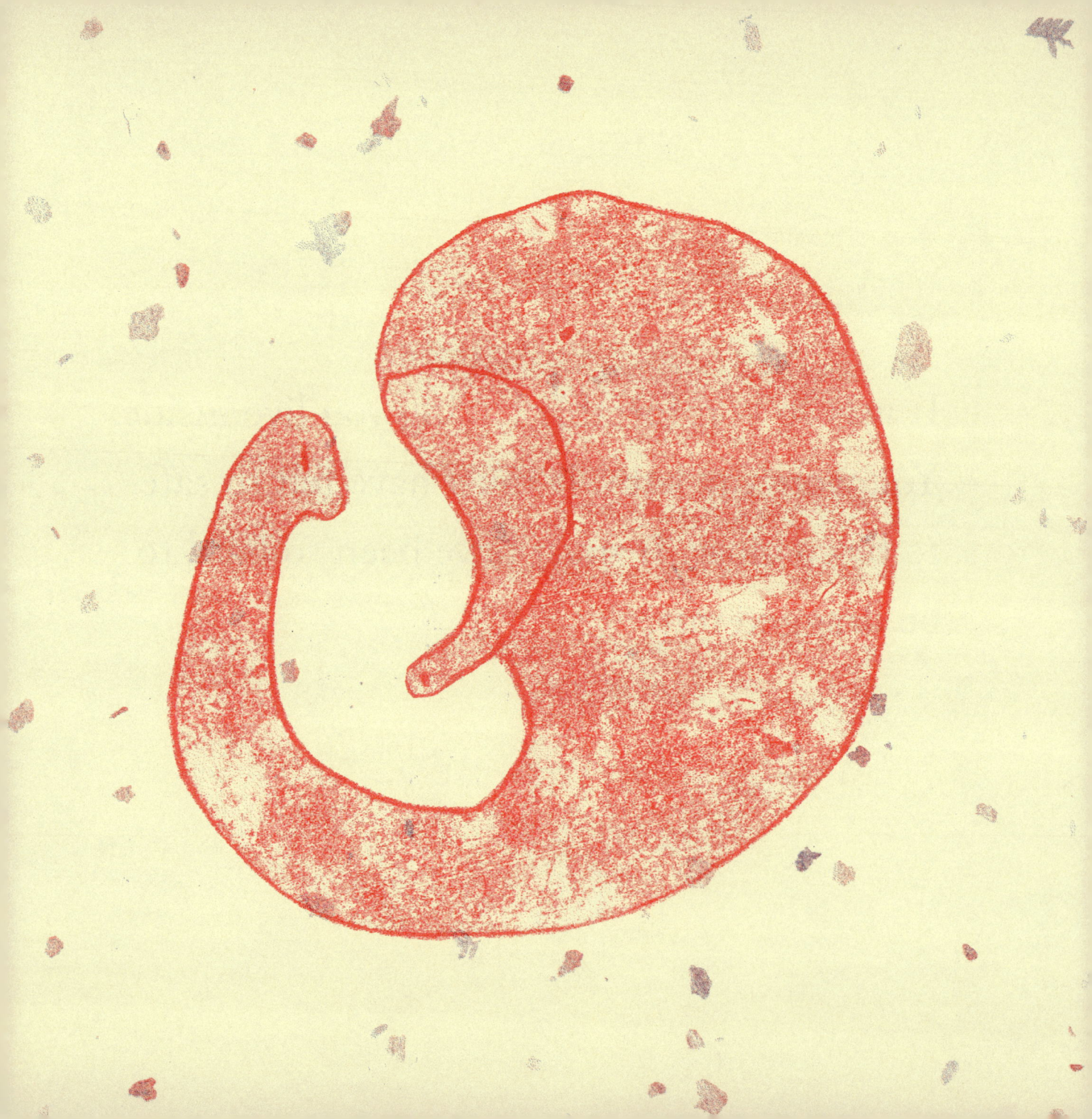

You came out through a slit in my tummy, and then I was gone.

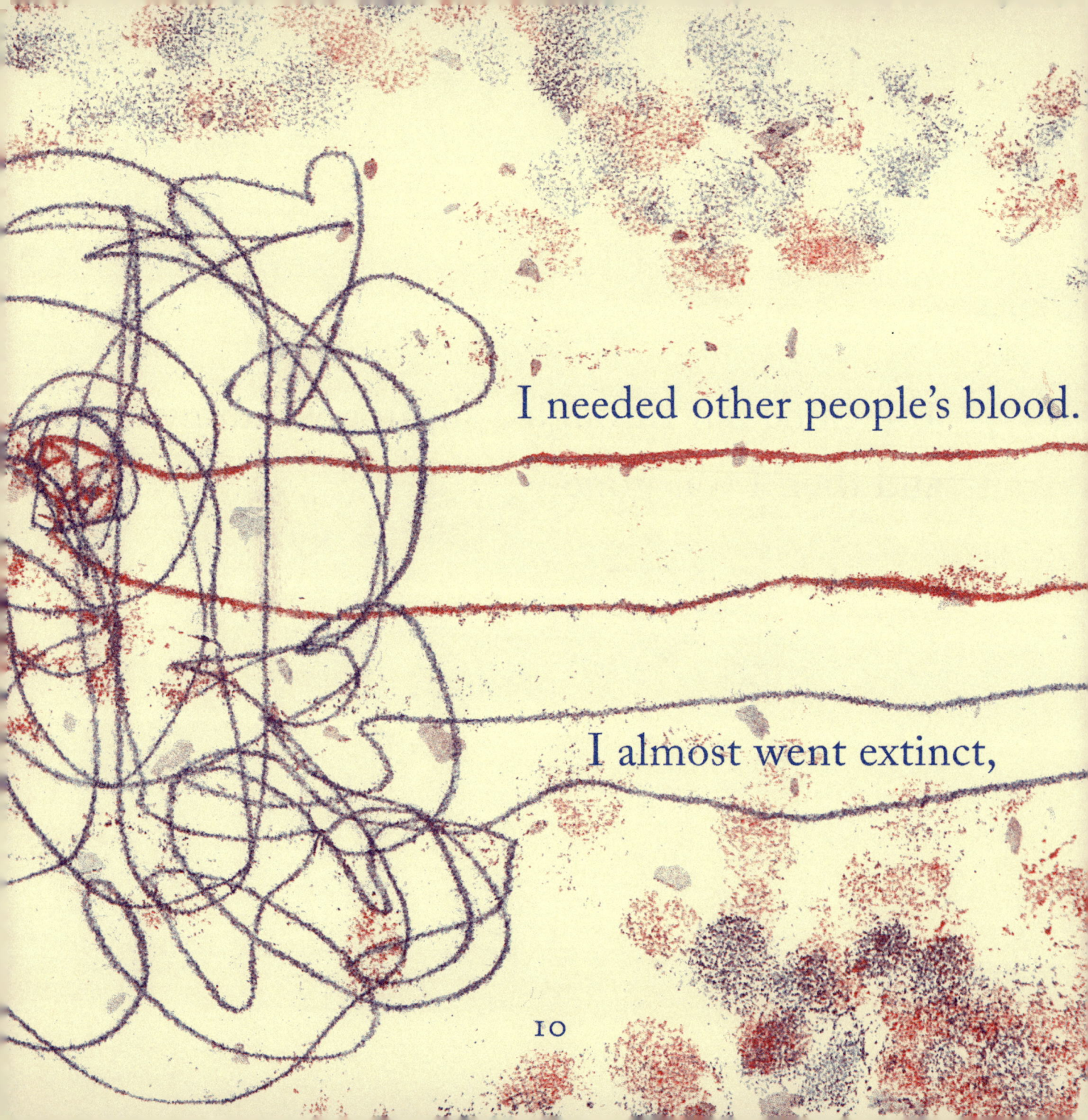

When I woke up I felt like I was missing. I had no idea who was lying there on the hospital bed, railings up, holding a newborn you.

I was holding my broken body and invisible lost body parts too. The Earth trembled from my heavy beating heart.

Other people's blood kept dripping and circling in me.

I was hurting.

You were growing.

I flinched, I stretched, I groaned, I screamed, I moaned, I failed.

I just couldn't.

I realized my heart was very small. The size of a pea, maybe. There was very little love inside, struggling to get out.

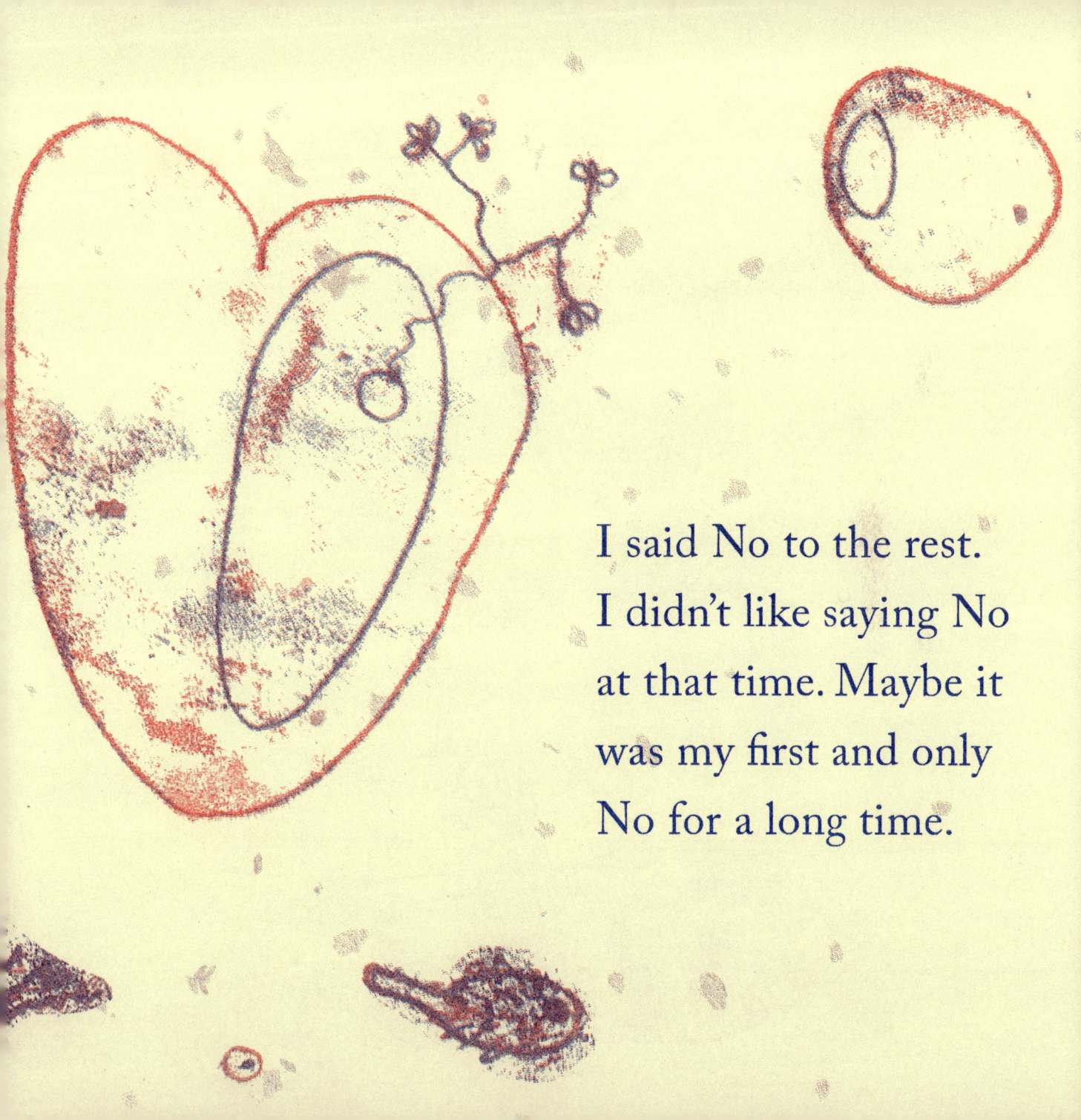

I said No to the rest. I didn't like saying No at that time. Maybe it was my first and only No for a long time.

Then my heart started to grow with you.
I made it grow so you got all the love you deserved.

Now I watch my heart. I check it every morning and every night so it doesn't stop growing with you.

Sometimes I put my hand on your heart at night as you fall asleep, and I imagine the cherry blossoms I saw near Tokyo Kiyosumi garden. My heart is full of cherry petals that fall from my heart to yours.

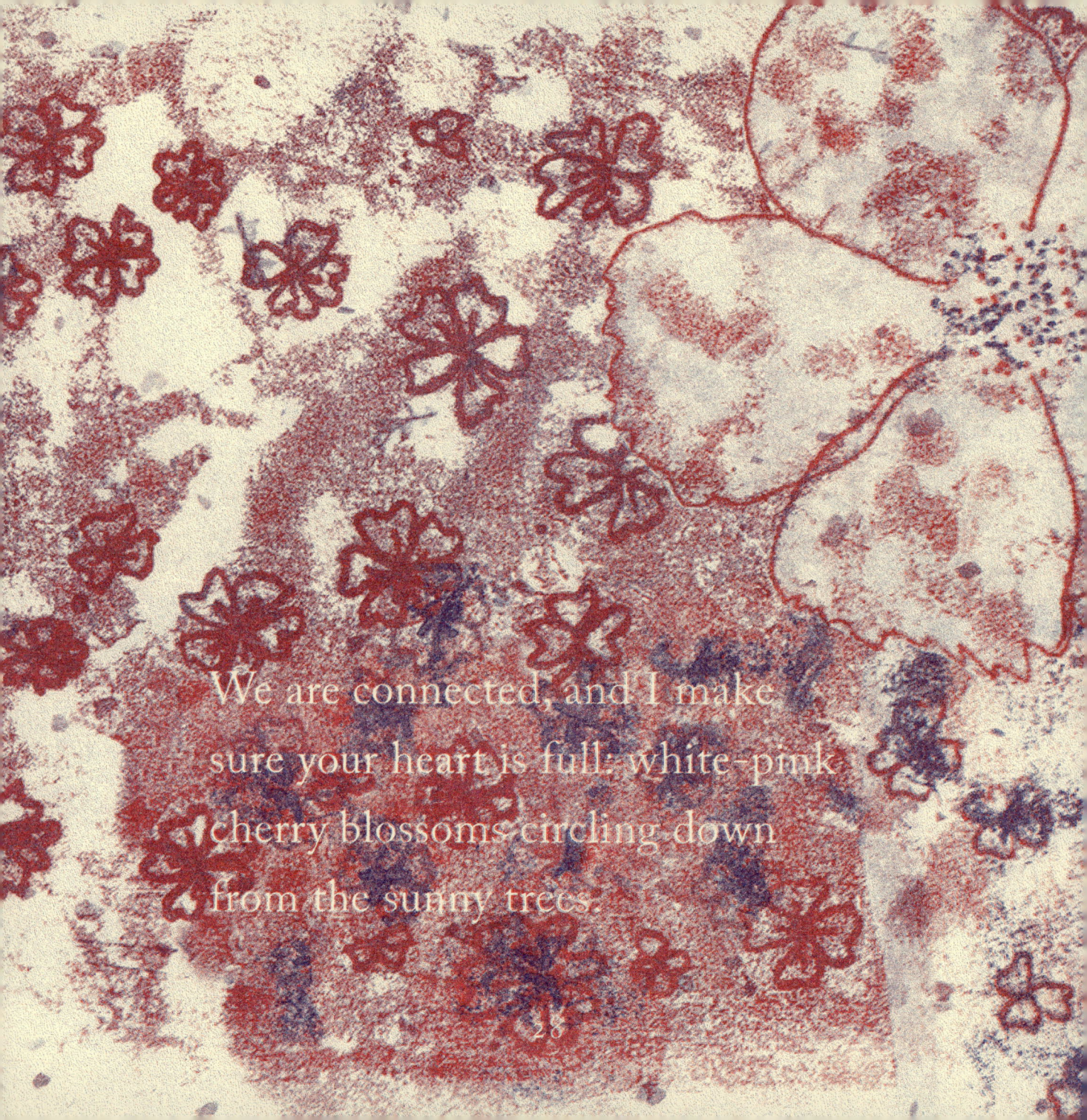

We are connected, and I make sure your heart is full: white-pink cherry blossoms circling down from the sunny trees.

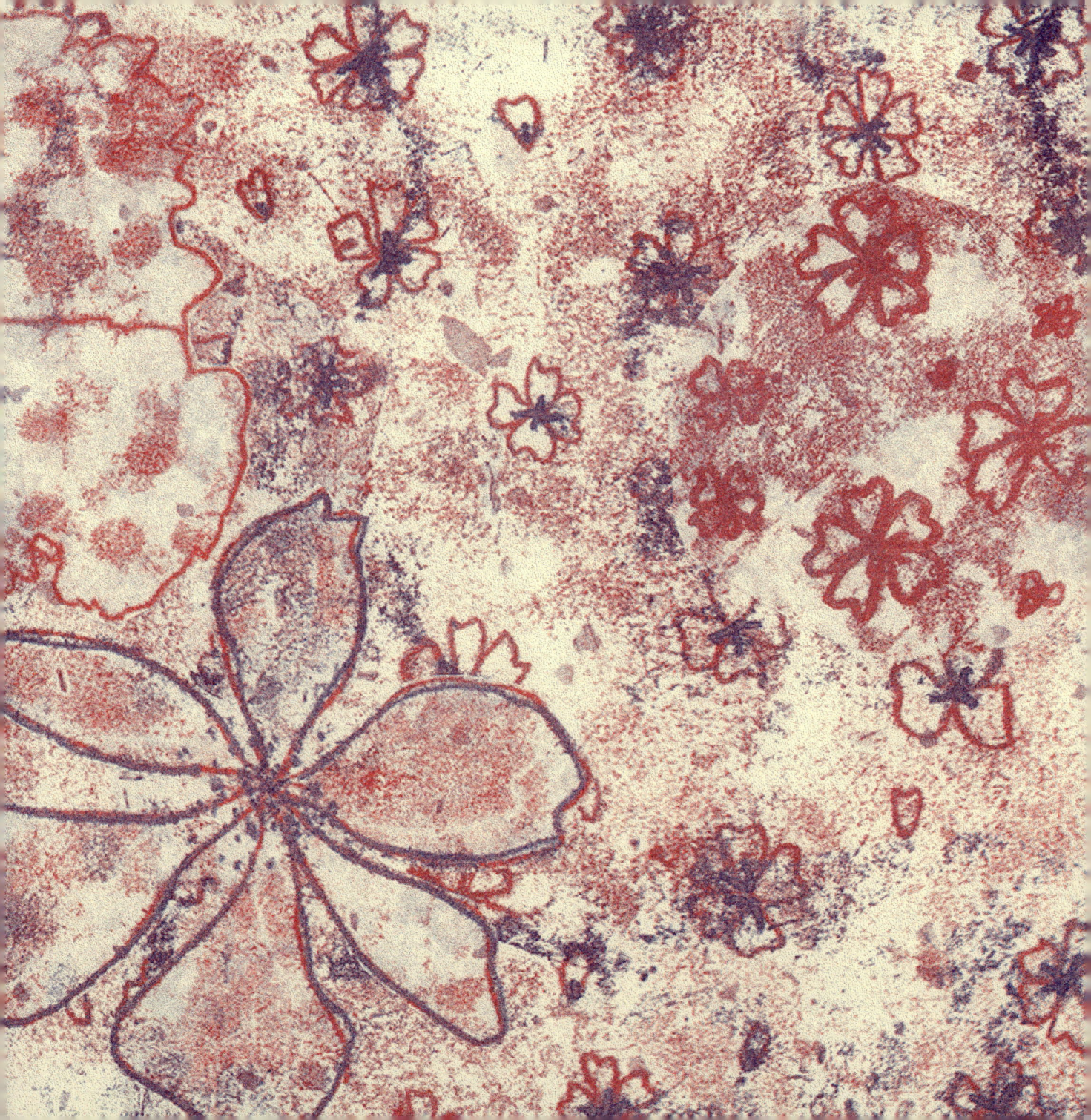

Today you made an anger pile: you threw our laundry, books, coins, toothbrushes, plastic animals and my wet rain jacket into a pile on the floor. You were so angry.

I said: *Make it as big as your anger.* You added chairs, seeds, more clothes, scissors and the Travel Taiwan book. At some point you started to laugh.

Later you were so proud of that pile, when we cleaned it all up. It was a good day.

I am so proud.

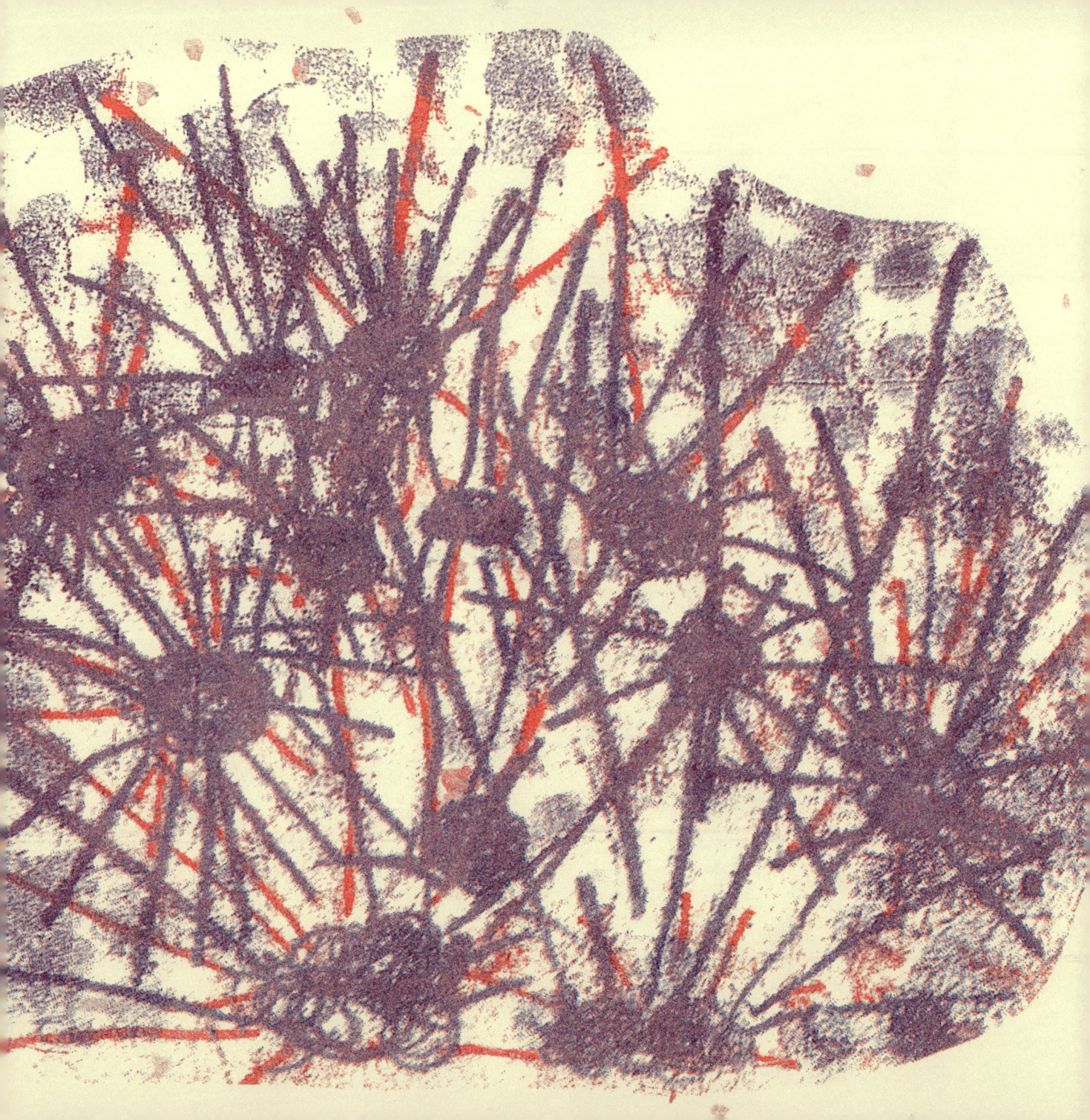

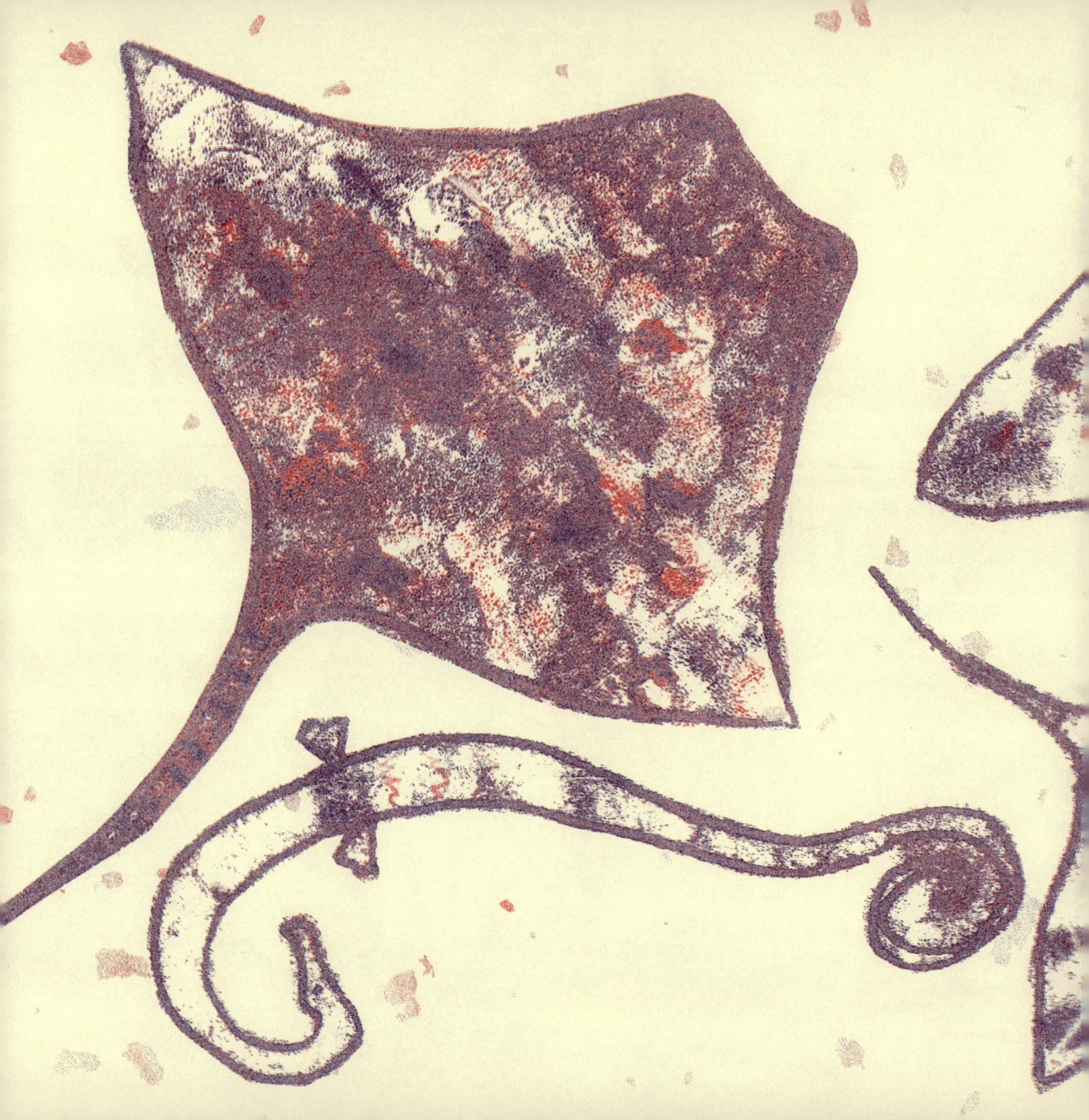

You say: *Look at me, I am breakdown dancing!* and *Stars have spread like chicken pox, and they create an upside-down triangle with the Moon that stings like a stingray.*

You wake up in the middle of the night and ask for a glass of water then dip your hand inside. You say your hand is full of sand.

I remember the back pains and endless headaches and tons of mommy guilt pressing down on my body.

You are safe.

You can.

We are changing the world right now, as we hold each other's hearts. Love.

Look at us: we are real dinosaurs! The Earth trembles when we laugh.

About the author

Elīna Eihmane is a Latvian artist, filmmaker, poet and mother, based in Taiwan. She writes gentle lullabies with patches of darkness, and creates handmade artist's books. Elīna writes to remember, to listen, and to live.

https://cargocollective.com/elinaeihmane

About The Emma Press

The Emma Press is an independent publisher dedicated to producing beautiful, thought-provoking books. It was founded in Winnersh in 2012 by Emma Dai'an Wright, and is now based in Birmingham. The Emma Press publishes anthologies, poetry and fiction chapbooks, and books for children, with a growing list of translations. It was awarded funding from Arts Council England in 2020 through the Elevate programme, for diverse-led arts organisations to build resilience.

https://theemmapress.com/

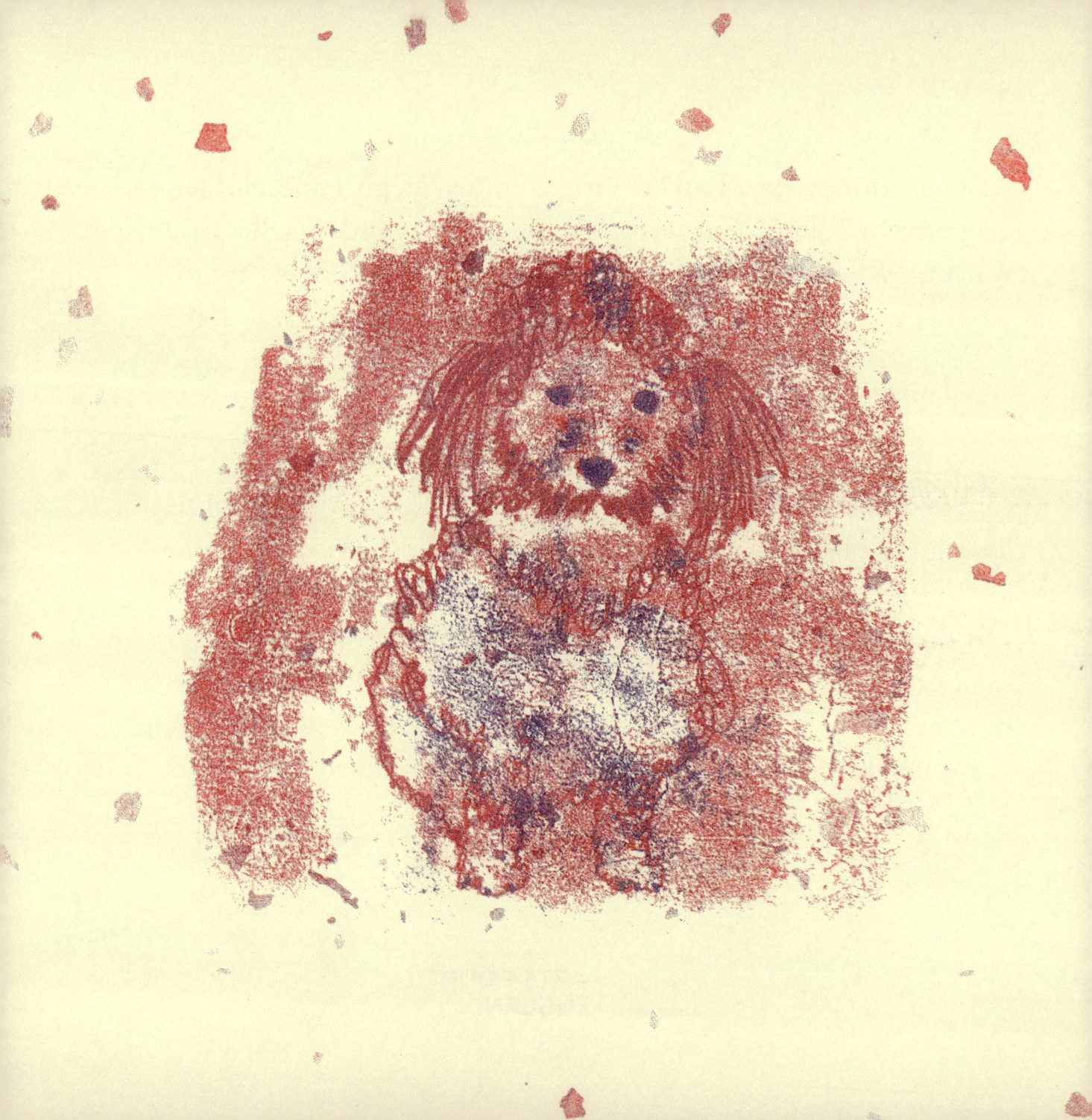